a morning cup of prayer® for women

CRANE HILL
PUBLISHERS

Published by Crane Hill Publishers
www.cranehill.com

Book design by Miles G. Parsons
Illustrations by Tim Rocks and Christena Brooks
Cover art by Christena Brooks

Printed in China

Library of Congress Cataloging-in-Publication Data

Bright-Fey, J. (John)
  A morning cup of prayer for women / John Bright-Fey. -- Crane Hill ed.
     p. cm.
  ISBN-13: 978-1-57587-266-7
  ISBN-10: 1-57587-266-8
  1. Christian women--Religious life. 2. Prayer--Christianity. 3. Prayers.
I. Title.
  BV4527.B727 2006
  248.3'2082--dc22
                          2006016163

a morning cup of prayer

for women

A daily guided devotional for a lifetime of inspiration and peace

john a. bright-fey

CRANE HILL
PUBLISHERS

Acknowledgments

I would like to thank the following individuals for their invaluable help and advice. This Morning Cup would surely not taste as sweet without their assistance:

To Professor Tom Gibbs for talking me into teaching college classes on prayer and contemplative living;
To all of my students whose experience of prayer and faith has profoundly moved me and deeply informed my work;
To Ellen, Linda, and all the staff and artists at Crane Hill Publishers for giving me this glorious opportunity;
To my amazing wife, Kim, who helps me in more ways than she could possibly know;
To the many men and women of faith that have, through the years, guided and shaped my life of prayer.

I thank God for each of you.

Dedication

In Loving Memory
Viola Gertrude Patricia Caverlee Marshall
"Grandma Vi"

Thanks for teaching me how to listen.

Contents

Let us then approach the throne of grace with confidence,
so that we may receive mercy and find grace to help us
in our time of need.
—*Hebrews 4:16*

Foreword

Would you, as a woman, like closer contact with God? If your answer is "Yes," then this book was written for you. With it you can come to know Him as never before. The means to begin this journey, and the power to sustain it for a lifetime are the same: prayer.

This *Morning Cup of Prayer* is designed to be a spiritual patchwork quilt of advice, wisdom, and inspiration for women of all ages. With it you will find peace with God as you surrender to His love through prayer.

The many issues confronting today's women are complex and varied. I've tried to write this book to be as inclusive and accessible as possible. As you give it your attention, consider it within the context of your own career, devotional path, and religious life.

I say that "I wrote" this book, but in truth my hand was guided by God and its contents formed by His Grace. I felt His love with every word. Now, it is my sincerest wish that you feel it, too.

Women and Prayer

There are so many women in the world today that, for many reasons, simply do not pray. This is a sad situation because so many of today's problems yield readily to prayer's power.

Prayer can change the course of an individual life or the life of a nation. Families torn apart by strife, disaster, or indifference can be made whole again with prayer. It can cure the worst physical illnesses and heal the deepest emotional wounds. If we become lost, it helps us to find our way again. Prayer knows. It pulls us back from the brink of what is toxic and shows us where and when to move forward toward nourishment. Most importantly, prayer is our birthright as God's children. It energizes, strengthens, comforts, informs, supports, and protects us. Simply put, prayer reclaims lives, futures, and souls.

With all that prayer has to offer, why then don't more women pray? The answer is simple: they don't know how.

Perhaps you are one of those individuals who needs the complete wholeness that prayer provides but are confused about the subject. Maybe you are in a mental or emotional fog and feel as though you just don't know how, when, or where to pray. The book you are now holding will solve those problems. It will help clear the path and show you the way to prayer.

I've divided this book into three parts. The first will be a discussion of the special needs of women that can be addressed by prayer. I have always felt that God favors women in matters of prayer. Our Savior Jesus Christ was a strong advocate of women. He celebrated and protected them. He treated them with the greatest respect. Yet, so many women have become mired in the conflicts and complexities of modern life. They have forgotten that Jesus was sent by our Father to save them as well as men. The key to remembering His promise is prayer.

The second part of this book will be a discussion of the mechanics of prayer and some of its methods. I will also discuss what a prayerful life can look like.

Most often when someone tells me, "I don't pray," what they are really saying is, "I don't know what to say to God." If you are one of those individuals, please don't worry. In the third part of this book, I will present you with an assortment of Biblically based prayers and relevant passages from His Word that both support and augment them. Each scriptural prayer was written especially with the needs of women in mind. They are grouped with the passages from scripture that, I believe, most women will find suitable for contemplation and prayer. Take your time as you read and study them. They bring much to the table.

Please look upon these prayers as suggestions. True prayer is a profoundly personal thing that must come from your heart. Think of the prayers and passages in this book as starting points for your personal spiritual journey. Use them to get comfortable with the act of praying. Then, as guided by the Holy Spirit, you will learn to speak the language of prayer.

In the time it would take for you to have a pleasant cup of tea, you can begin your spiritual journey and sustain it for a lifetime. Indeed, heartfelt prayer is ambrosia that, once tasted, will change every woman's life for the better. Would you like to share a Morning Cup with me?

JBF
Birmingham, Alabama
2006

For the eyes of the Lord are on the righteous and his ears
are attentive to their prayer, but the face of the Lord is
against those who do evil.
—1 Peter 3:12

Why Women Need Prayer

The Noble Woman

A wife of noble character who can find?
She is worth far more than rubies.

Her husband has full confidence in her
and lacks nothing of value.

She brings him good, not harm,
all the days of her life.

She selects wool and flax
and works with eager hands.

She is like the merchant ships,
bringing her food from afar.

She gets up while it is still dark;
she provides food for her family
and portions for her servant girls.

She considers a field and buys it;
out of her earnings she plants a vineyard.

She sets about her work vigorously;
her arms are strong for her tasks.

She sees that her trading is profitable,
and her lamp does not go out at night.

In her hand she holds the distaff
and grasps the spindle with her fingers.

She opens her arms to the poor
and extends her hands to the needy.

When it snows, she has no fear for her household;
for all of them are clothed in scarlet.

She makes coverings for her bed;
she is clothed in fine linen and purple.

Her husband is respected at the city gate,
where he takes his seat among the elders of the land.

She makes linen garments and sells them,
and supplies the merchants with sashes.

She is clothed with strength and dignity;
she can laugh at the days to come.

She speaks with wisdom,
and faithful instruction is on her tongue.

She watches over the affairs of her household
and does not eat the bread of idleness.

Her children arise and call her blessed;
her husband also, and he praises her:

"Many women do noble things,
but you surpass them all."

Charm is deceptive, and beauty is fleeting;
but a woman who fears the LORD is to be praised.

Give her the reward she has earned,
and let her works bring her praise at the city gate.

—Proverbs 31:10-31

When I first encountered the thirty-first Proverb, it immediately struck me that the qualities of the Noble Wife were those positive qualities that God placed in all women. It also struck me that it would be a daunting task for any modern woman to live up to.

So many trials and hardships confront women. In the face of modern culture, trying to live up to the standard set by Proverbs 31 seems well nigh impossible. But Jesus came to save women as well as men. In doing so, He put the impossible within our reach.

And I will do whatever you ask in my name, so that the Son may bring glory to the Father. You may ask me for anything in my name, and I will do it.
—*John 14:13-14*

I believe that, when guided by the Holy Spirit, each of us knows full well the extent of our gifts and our deficits. We intrinsically know what to do to conquer our fears and address those issues that stand between us and our being the person God knows us to be. We have but to do it.

But what are the issues confronting today's woman? What are those problems that the gift of prayer can address? Here is a partial list:

- Feeling overwhelmed
- Taking the weight of the world on your shoulders
- Learning to care for others while still caring for yourself
- Learning when and how to say, "no"
- Depression
- Abuse
- Learning to appreciate the good things in life
- Anger
- Being a "Superwoman" who can do anything
- Feeling trapped in a job or relationship
- Having purpose in life

- Letting yourself have fun
- Negative self image
- Feeling isolated and abandoned
- Letting people know who you really are
- Feeling taken for granted
- Feeling alone
- Feeling tired

Surely, I could continue but these issues seem to be the ones most commonly expressed by women. Perhaps you have experienced one or more of these conditions in your life. Perhaps you are experiencing them now. If you are, then it's time to take the key of prayer and through Christ Jesus enter your Father's house to seek His wisdom. If you can pray authentically, that is from your heart, then you will be shown how to overcome these or any problems. It's as simple as that.

What Is Prayer?

The stated goal of this book is to teach women how to pray. In order to do that, we need a definition of precisely what "praying" is. We also need to discuss the different kinds of prayer and the best ways to approach them. Before we get much further, though, I have a story that might help us get things off to a good start and insure a great finish. I think every woman will be able to relate to it.

A Woman's Example of Prayer

My inspiration for this book on prayer and the model I use for conducting a prayerful life come from a woman very dear to me.

Everything I know about prayer I learned from my maternal grandmother, Viola. Grandma Vi was a devout churchgoer and easily the most amazing Christian that you'd ever be likely to meet. To be fair, I've learned a lot about prayer, contemplation, and devotion from many other wonderful men and women of faith. But the lessons from Grandma remain to this day the most profound, direct, and the most useful that I've ever received. Everything she did—whether it was homemaking, teaching music, comforting a friend or being a wife and grandmother—she approached with prayer.

Every morning after putting away the breakfast dishes, Grandma Vi would quietly announce that she was going to her room to "talk with God." She would then retire to the back bedroom, close the door, and do precisely that. Forty-five minutes to an hour later, she would emerge renewed, refreshed—transformed really—confident, self assured, and positively radiant.

No matter what difficulties life presented her, the negative would literally fade away as her smile and countenance pushed back the gloom. The grace she radiated was as palpable and real as gravity. You could feel it; you could almost hold it in your hand. No matter what kind of ugly mood had you by the scruff of the neck, her smile set you free. Grandma had just finished talking with God and everything was, profoundly, right with the world.

Talking with God

I cannot remember how young I was when I first realized that Grandma said, "talk with God" instead of the usual "talk to God" that most people say when discussing prayer. Indeed, the transformation that would occur within her bespoke of something much more than simply a one-sided long distance conversation. I mean, it looked like she and God had actually been sitting in her room having a chat!

When I asked her what she and God talked about, she would reply, "Oh, all kinds of things." "Big stuff?" I asked. "Yes," she said "but, small things, too. I ask Him to watch over you and the rest of the family. If I have a problem I ask for His help and the strength to take care of it the way that He wants me to. I thank Him for all of the happiness and blessings He has given me. Most of the time, though, God talks and I listen to Him. You have to listen if you're going to have a real conversation with God. He likes it when we listen, just the way I like it when you listen to me. After all, He loves me the way that I love you."

"Do you only talk to God in your room?" I asked. "No," she said. "He meets me here." As she spoke she touched my heart with her hand. "I talk with Him here." That made me feel good and I remember thinking in a child's way that while it was important to love God, it was far more important to let Him love you.

Look to the Lord and his strength; seek his face always.
—*Psalm 105:4*

Any Time, Any Place, Any Thing, Any Subject

As I grew older, my fascination with prayer grew, as did my love for God. Yes, our relationship had its rocky moments, but pop culture and arrogant churchmen aside, I never lost contact with Him or forgot how important it was to surrender to His Grace.

Grandma Vi continued to amaze me with her gifts of prayer. When I would drive the twelve hours from college to my grandparents' trailer in Bossier City, Louisiana, she would, quite literally, pray me in. Think about it; she would go about her daily chores with half of her attention actively engaged in a twelve-hour-long continuous prayer for my safe journey. Frequently, she'd have a "message from God" for me when I arrived at the trailer, along with a warm embrace and a home cooked meal that was fit for, well, Jehovah.

Later, when I was rested and ready to drive the additional three hours to home, she would smile and say, "Be careful and be sure to call me when you get to your Mom's house so I know when to quit praying." No matter what time it was, she wouldn't go to sleep until she'd received my call.

I have no doubt that even after I called the trailer to let her know of my safe arrival, she continued to pray. It was clear to me that her whole life was a prayer. That was what I wanted for myself and, over the years, it became what I wanted for everyone else.

Grandma made it plain; a person could—and should—have a heartfelt conversation with God anytime, anywhere, under any circumstances, and about anything.

Different Kinds of Prayer

Grandma's prayers on my behalf were an example of Intercessory prayer, where one person prays for another. There are other kinds of prayer as well.

There are prayers of Thanksgiving and of Praise where we thank our Heavenly Father for the blessings He has given us and give honor to His Grace and Perfect Will. We can obtain more of God through Seeking prayer wherein we simply announce our intention to rest in His presence and allow Him to speak through His Word. Prayers of Confession allow you to repent your sins and ask your Father for the blessing of His forgiveness. Prayers of Supplication involve asking God for His Divine intervention. Submissive prayer or prayers of Surrender involve completely opening up to God's love and welcoming His Grace and Will into our lives.

Different Ways to Pray

Just as there are different kinds of prayer, there are also different ways to pray. You may talk with God silently or aloud. You may mindfully and deliberately repeat passages from the Bible while pondering the meaning of His Word. This is called Repetitive prayer. Prayer can be performed Reflectively by sitting still and coming to know God through the peace of silence or by reflecting on the deeper meaning of His hand at work in your life.

The Most Important Thing about Prayer

Don't let the different kinds of prayer or the different ways to pray confuse you. Remember Grandma Vi's model:

You talk with God (that means listening as well as talking)

- Anytime,
- Anywhere,
- (under) Any circumstances,
- (about) Anything.
- ?

But something is missing. What's vitally important is that your prayers be authentic, that is, they must come from your heart and be in your own voice. Even if you are reading a Biblically based prayer composed by someone else, you must make it real for you. You must see it, feel it, taste it, and touch it with everything you've got. So now we have our final "A": Authentically.

You Talk With God

- Anytime
- Anywhere
- Any Circumstances
- Anything
- Authentically

...if my people, who are called by my name, will humble themselves and pray and seek my face and turn from their wicked ways, then will I hear from heaven and will forgive their sin and will heal their land.
—2 Chronicles 7:14

Why Should Women Pray?

There are so many good reasons for women to pray. To start with, reread the list on page 20-21. All of those problems and circumstances can be addressed and solved with prayer. But there are other reasons as well. You can pray:

- for spiritual growth
- for material needs
- for protection from evil
- to confess your sins and ask for forgiveness
- for the sins of others
- for the needs of others
- for the church and its missions
- for others to receive His Word

- for personal healing
- for others to be healed
- for wisdom about any subject
- to help simplify your life
- for personal direction
- to participate in His holy work around the world

The list could go on forever. When it comes to prayer, you are only as limited as your imagination.

I tell you the truth, my Father will give you whatever you ask in my name. Until now you have not asked for anything in my name. Ask and you will receive, and your joy will be complete.
—John 16:23-24

Prayer is a wonderful gift from our Heavenly Father. He places great value on it and we should avail ourselves of it. So much can be accomplished through the power of prayer. You have but to read the stories of Moses, Samson, Elijah, and the apostle Peter in the Bible to grasp its potential.*

Yet, so often, we feel like we don't have the time or the energy for prayer. Many of us lead such busy lives. Our minds and our bodies work overtime to accomplish the many things we must in order to fulfill our earthly obligations. But when we stop to pray, even if only for a few moments, our whole being changes. We slow our frantic pace, focus on God, and say, "Lord, I love you with all my heart and soul."

Whenever anyone asks me why they should pray, rather than listing the reasons, I say this: "Your Heavenly Father loves you dearly and wants you to visit with Him often. He wants you to come to Him for rest, advice, encouragement, and all manner of council. You can visit anytime you want, day or night. Calling ahead isn't necessary because He is always home waiting for you, His beloved child. There amid the beats of His heart, you will surely find nourishment, comfort, and joy. You will find meaning and direction. If you come to Him when you are sick, He will heal you. No matter how many people are cruel to you or how much life has beaten you down, you can always go to your Father's home. You can tell Him anything and He will be there for you. All you have to do is show up. The doorway to His heart is His son Jesus Christ and the key to that doorway is prayer." Now that sounds like a reason enough for me. How about you?

*Moses (Exodus 15:24-26); Samson (Judges 16:28-30); Elijah (James 5:17,18); Peter (Acts 9:36-41).

The Lord is near to all who call upon him, to all who call on him in truth.
—*Psalm 145:18*

And pray in the Spirit on all occasions with all kinds of prayers and requests. With this in mind, be alert and always keep on praying for all the saints.
—*Ephesians 6:18*

How Women Should Pray

*But when you pray, go into your room, close the door
and pray to your Father, who is unseen. Then your
Father, who sees what is done in secret, will reward you.*
—Matthew 6:6

Step One:
Set The Stage With Solitude, Silence, and Stillness

Do you remember how Grandma Vi would go into her room to
pray? She was following the instructions laid out in Matthew 6:6.
It's the very first thing you should do before you pray: find a place
of solitude and enter it.

Your place of solitude can be a room or the corner of a room. It
can be your back porch. In truth, it doesn't even have to be a
physical structure. Your place of solitude can be out of doors in the
deep woods or a even a public park filled with people. It can be any
place where you can engineer a feeling of being alone.

When you enter into solitude you enter into the realm of the
soul. Here, God gives you the opportunity to drop all pretense and
simply be yourself. When you are in solitude you are never really
alone. You and your Heavenly Father are there together. That is His
promise.

After entering into the realm of the soul, you should then embrace silence and stillness. Here's how you do it.

Generally relax, accept the guidance of the Holy Spirit and tell yourself that you are preparing for prayer, preparing to talk with God. Close your eyes and briefly watch your body and how it naturally moves. For example, your chest rises and falls as you breathe. That's okay; just let it. Perhaps you notice some tension in your neck so you gently drop your shoulders downward a bit to release it. If you notice any physical movement at all, just take notice of it and say to yourself that you'd like to sit as still as you are comfortably able.

You may find it helpful to have soothing music accompany your preparations for prayer. If so, you will enjoy the Morning Cup Audio CD that accompanies this volume. It was designed especially to set the tone for your prayer time.

Turn your attention to your mind. Other than focusing on God and your intention to pray, don't try to control it in any way. Try not to chastise yourself for a wandering mind that jumps around in the background from one mental topic to the next. Simply acknowledge that your mind is doing something, casually watch it unfold, and keep your focus on your Father and His presence.

Settling into a time of prayer may be like watching a river flow by out of the corner of your eye. You'll notice obvious things like sailboats, motor craft, tree limbs floating on the surface, even the occasional duck. There are birds flying above the river and fish you cannot see swimming beneath its surface. You're sitting in one place with God but all of the life that is the river flows past you. Enjoy yourself. After all, you are preparing to talk with God. What could be better than that?

Put a light smile on your face as you allow the river of your mind to float by and you'll begin to notice something: your mind will settle down, your body will relax, and you will begin to feel quiet all over. Sometimes it feels as if you are sensing all of your parts all at once. The best word I know of to describe your sensation is "quiescence." Every part of you settles down and you will feel organized and peaceful. You become bathed in God's Grace and Presence. Now you are ready. This is the canvas upon which you will present your prayers.

It Only Takes A Moment

Though you could spend a lot of time completing your preparations for prayer, it really only takes a moment to engineer solitude, silence, and stillness. With practice you'll be able to set the stage for prayer in an instant.

There is benefit in setting the stage and resting in the realm of the soul for longer periods of time. In this way you utilize solitude, silence, and stillness to reflect and listen for God's wisdom and guidance. There in His loving embrace, you will experience genuine tranquility and perfect peace of mind.

Step Two:
Embrace A Prayerful Attitude

Prayer is so very much more than mere words. It is an attitude that reflects our most heartfelt wishes and hopes. In reality, it's all about heart—your heart to God's heart.

We are all God's children. As a parent He isn't gruff or unfeeling, yet we often approach Him as if He is. Our Father is love itself and the secret to true prayer is simple: we must be His children.

I often ask people who pray regularly to listen to themselves as they pray. "Try it for yourself," I say. "How do you sound when you pray? Do you sound like an outsider intruding upon God's quiet repose? Do you plead or beg? Do your words impose or do you sound like a child talking with a beloved parent?"

That last example, of course, is how it should be. We should not sound like spiritual panhandlers. We are God's loving and obedient children and behaving in that way is the secret key to true and authentic prayer.

We Are Unique

In His wisdom, our Heavenly Father created each of us to be a unique individual. When He gave us the gift of prayer He knew that each of us would have our own unique way of speaking with Him. That's precisely the way He wants it. He wants each of us to be completely honest and authentic by expressing what's in our heart to Him. Remember, whether you offer spontaneous prayers or prayers composed by someone else, you must feel it in your heart.

 Step Three:
Choose Your Method of Prayer

There are many ways that you can pray. For this Morning Cup I've chosen four ways that you may engage in prayer:

Spoken Prayer

Simply put, speak aloud. Declaiming your prayers out loud has a special quality to it. When you taste what you are saying, the words have a greater effect upon you and your prayers become powerful.

Silent Prayer

Silent prayers are more intimate than spoken ones. Praying in this way brings a delicate and private quality to your worship. Use silent prayer whenever you feel the need to more personally connect with your Heavenly Father.

Repetitive Prayer

Repeat your prayer over and over. You may do this aloud or silently in your mind. However, no matter how you choose to say the prayer, it is important that each repetition be mindful and deliberate. Mindlessly repeating words is not praying. Repetitive, authentic prayer produces a profoundly focused communication with God.

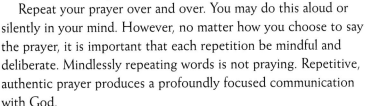

Reflective Prayer

Reflective prayer is performed in silence. Simply read a Biblical passage or any prayer that you choose and silently reflect on its meaning. Just hold the thought of the prayer in your heart and mind. The Holy Spirit does the rest. Reflective prayer engenders peaceful communication with God and reveals His Wisdom.

Step Four:
Talk with God

All of the prayers that make up the balance of this book have been composed, and the Bible selections chosen, with the idea of using them in any one of the above prayer methods outlined in Step Three. Of course, you can dispense with them altogether and speak with your Father according to the dictates of your heart. But what if you have never prayed before?

Do you remember my comments in the introduction about people who say that they don't know how to pray? All too often, they really just don't know what to say to God. If you are one of those people then you probably remember that I also told you not to worry.

The next section of this book contains all the suggestions you need to learn how to speak the language of prayer. Please learn from it and let it inspire you to lead a prayerful life. Your Father is in His home and He would dearly love to speak with you.

Step Five:
Listen to God

The fifth and final step of prayer is probably the most important. At least it was for Grandma Vi. Do you remember what she said about how she spent most of her prayer time? That's right; she spent it listening.

Please remember, authentic prayer is a conversation filled with devotion and love that takes place between you and your Heavenly Father. Prayer is so incredibly precious to God. It releases an enormous outpouring of His wisdom, power, inspiration, and strength. But you have to listen and you have to listen patiently.

After speaking to Him, ask God to speak back to you in any way He sees fit. You may use the journal that begins on page 71 to record any important thoughts and insights that come up, especially when He speaks to you through His Word. Let Him call your attention to those areas in your life where He wants to help.

Spend as much time listening to God as you would like. One minute of really listening to God would be great. Fifteen would be so much better. You choose. An hour listening to God isn't too much, and neither is a lifetime.

Let us then labor for an inward stillness,
An inward stillness and an inward healing;
That perfect silence where lips and heart
Are still, and we no longer entertain
Our own imperfect thoughts and vain opinions,
But God alone speaks in us, and we wait
In singleness of heart, that we may know
God's will, and in the silence of our spirit,
That we may do God's will and do that only.
—Longfellow, The Christus

A Woman's Life Inspired by Prayer

I've always loved the word "inspired." It means, "in-spirit." When my publisher approached me to write several books on prayer for the Morning Cup series she could hardly have known that on those mornings after my grandmother had chatted with God, she would, invariably, make a cup of tea, sit down, leisurely sip, and bask in the glow of being "in spirit." I can think of no better way to start a day or spend a life. Can you?

The Lord's Prayer

This, then, is how you should pray:
" Our Father in heaven,
hallowed be your name,

your kingdom come,
your will be done
on earth as it is in heaven.

Give us today our daily bread.
Forgive us our debts,
as we also have forgiven our debtors.

And lead us not into temptation,
but deliver us from the evil one."
—Matthew 6:9-13

Prayers for Women

Whenever the demands of being a woman in today's world make you feel tense, nervous, and uncertain, it is time to surrender through prayer. Authentic prayer is a fundamental rededication of your faith every time you engage in it. It brings the peace of the Father to you by helping you to completely open up to His love, wisdom, strength, and forgiveness.

Relax your heart and bring peace to your soul by surrendering all of your cares and worries to God through prayer. What doubts could you possibly have when you are resting in your Father's loving arms while being filled with His Grace?

Prayers

As you begin to incorporate prayer into your life, you may find it helpful to have examples of prayers to get you started. Here are some samples that, along with selected scripture passages, will set the tone for prayer. As you make these initial steps, the Holy Spirit will help you in your efforts.

A Prayer for Direction

Father, in the name of Jesus, I surrender to the Holy Spirit. Fill my soul with Your Grace and let me lead the life that You have set out for me. Amen.

This is what the Lord says—your Redeemer, the Holy One of Israel: "I am the Lord your God, who teaches you what is best for you, who directs you in the way you should go."
—Isaiah 48:17

A Prayer for Guidance

Heavenly Father, I submit to the guiding wisdom of the Holy Spirit. I will open up and receive its power as directed by Your Divine Will. Amen.

When the Counselor comes, whom I will send to you from the Father, the Spirit of truth who goes out from the Father, he will testify about me.
—John 15:26

All that the Father gives me will come to me, and whoever comes to me I will never drive away.
—John 6:37

A Prayer for Wisdom

Today, O Lord, I need Your guidance and wisdom. Help me to comprehend the complexities of life that are now assailing me. Amen.

The light shines in the darkness, but the darkness has not understood it.
—*John 1:5*

The fear of the Lord is the beginning of wisdom; all who follow his precepts have good understanding. To him belongs eternal praise."
—*Psalm 111:10*

A Prayer for Renewal

Father, I surrender to a new way of thinking:
Your Way. Let my thoughts be cleansed and
organized. Let my attitudes align with Yours so
that I will know Your Perfect Will. Then, with
Your Grace, I will be renewed; then, I will be
transformed. Amen.

Wash me, and I will be whiter than snow.
—Psalm 51:7

Do not conform any longer to the pattern of this world,
but be transformed by the renewing of your mind. Then
you will be able to test and approve what God's will
is—his good, pleasing and perfect will.
—Romans 12:2

A Prayer of Surrender

Father, I surrender all of my cares and all of my
worries to You. Show me the way that reveals
Your Grace and wisdom. In Your arms I know
that I can handle any situation. Amen.

My slanderers pursue me all day long;
many are attacking me in their pride.
—Psalm 56:2

Cast all your anxiety on him because he cares for you.
—1 Peter 5:67

A Prayer for Comfort

Father, sometimes I become confused by what
seems to be the unfairness of life. But, resting
within the steady heartbeat of Your love, I always
will find solace and peace. Thank You for Your
many miracles and Your gift of my life.
Lord God, I fully open myself to Your Perfect
Will. Help me be a fit receptacle for Your Word
and allow Your gift of the Holy Spirit to abide
within my heart and soul. Amen.

Above all else, guard your heart,
for it is the wellspring of life.
—*Proverbs* 4:23

A Prayer for Forgiveness

Father, since You watch over me You know that my heart has been broken by someone I cared for deeply. Help me to not be bitter and—as You would want—forgive. I know that it will take time for the pain of rejection to go away. I also know that the gift of the Holy Spirit will guide me to peace and emotional healing. In Jesus' name, Amen.

For if you forgive men when they sin against you, your heavenly father will also forgive you. But if you do not forgive men their sins, your father will not forgive your sins.
—Matthew 6:14-15

A Prayer for Strength

Lord, I open myself to Your aid and mercy for I
have given myself over to fear. Even though I
know the fear to be false, it has caused me to be
hesitant and to misstep. I am heartedly sorry for
behaving in this way. Father, I know that I am
Your child and that You have made me strong
and courageous. Help me to honor my strength,
which flows from You. I know that which
intimidates me only appears real. You are the
One reality in whom I take refuge. With You by
my side I will stay the course and act firmly and
resolutely in accord with Your wishes. In Jesus'
name I pray, Amen.

A Prayer for Peace

Father, please help me turn away from
unwarranted contention and conflict. Let me
follow the example of Your Son Christ Jesus and
live in peace with everyone I meet so that I may
extend the goodness of Your love to them.
Amen.

Do not accuse a man for no reason
when he has done you no harm.
—Proverbs 3:30

If it is possible, as far as it depends on you, live at peace
with everyone.
—Romans 12:18

A Prayer for Acceptance

Dearest Lord, help me to accept those that I
cannot change and instead open myself to the
transforming power of the Holy Spirit. Grant me
Your Divine wisdom so that I may walk
peacefully in the company of others and
remember that they are my brothers and sisters.
Amen.

How great is the love the Father has lavished on us, that we should be called children of God! And that is what we are! The reason the world does not know us is that it did not know him.
—1 John 3:1

Above all else, guard your heart, for it is the wellspring of life.
—Proverbs 4:23

Both the one who makes men holy and those who are made holy are of the same family. So Jesus is not ashamed to call them brothers.
—Hebrews 2:11

A Prayer of Thanks

Father, I have so much to be thankful for. Thank
You for loving me as I am. Thank You for sending
Your Son Jesus to save me. Thank You for the
gift of the Holy Spirit which guides me
unerringly along Your path. And, thank You for
the gift of my life so that I may do Your Divine
Will. Amen.

An Extra Sip

Prayerwalking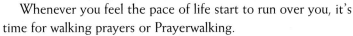

Whenever you feel the pace of life start to run over you, it's time for walking prayers or Prayerwalking.

Every time you take a step you have the opportunity for prayer. In many ways, walking prayers can have more impact on you than standing, kneeling, or sitting while you pray. This is because your entire body is in motion when you walk just as it is when you are going about your daily tasks. It is instrumental in teaching you how to pray during any activity and, eventually, to pray without ceasing.

Prayerwalking intrinsically reminds us of our connection to God's miracle, that is the earth. When we walk we feel it beneath our feet. We know it with our whole body just as we know about our Heavenly connection to our Father through our souls. Walking prayers enliven your senses, clear your thinking, and can energize you to God's Word. If you ever need reaffirmation of your chosen path in life or if you are having a hard time standing your ground for what you believe in, then pray as you walk.

Walking prayers are best done when you are alone. Anywhere you can walk slowly and deliberately will be suitable for these prayers. I prefer the outdoors, be it a city park, the woods, or your backyard. The choice is yours. It is important to bring a sense of stillness to your walk.

Pretend that the prayers are delicate and that a hurried pace might break them. Be gentle with yourself. As you walk among the many gifts that He has placed for us in this world, know that each step you take brings you closer to Him.

If you choose to walk in a public place, be sure not to call attention to what you are doing. But take the opportunity to pray for people you see along the way. If you pass someone who is obviously ill, then pray for them. If you see someone giving into sin, pray for their deliverance. You can walk around your home, garden, campus, or city hall and bring the power of prayer with you everywhere. Simply, walk and talk with God.

Walking Prayers

I walk with God in peace and contentment.
I walk with God and recognize His gifts to
  me.
I walk with God and am nourished by His
  loving kindness.
I walk with God and am healed and
  strengthened by His Grace.
I walk with God and extend His love to
  everyone.
I walk with God knowing that He is with me
  always.
I walk with God and am filled with the Holy
  Spirit.
I walk with God and breathe in His mercy.
I walk with God knowing His Perfect Will.
I walk with God upon a bedrock of His Word
  and bring the light of His message to the
  world.
In Jesus' name I pray, Amen.

A Prayer for God's Presence

Heavenly Father, please help me to walk in Your wisdom and grace. With every step I take, may I feel Your presence and know that You are my constant companion.

You are worthy, our Lord and God,
to receive glory and honor and power,
for you created all things,
and by your will they were created
and have their being.
—Revelation 4:11

Commit to the LORD whatever you do,
and your plans will succeed.
—Proverbs 16:3

Come, O house of Jacob, let us walk in the light of the Lord.
—Isaiah 2:5

An Affirmation of God's Power

Even though we may walk in divine silence, each footfall acknowledges Your power; each step shows me the difference between Your Heavenly truth and earthly pain. And as I walk, please know that I am Your devoted child.

In his heart a man plans his course,
but the LORD determines his steps.
—Proverbs 16:9

But if we walk in the light, as he is in the light, we
have fellowship with one another, and the blood of Jesus,
his Son, purifies us from all sin.
—1 John 1:7

A Prayer for Leadership

Father, Your gift of the Holy Spirit guides me as
I walk through Your gift of this life. Help my
soul to be refreshed and lead me to Your Word
and wondrous mystery.

Blessed are those who have learned to acclaim you, who
walk in the light of your presence, O Lord.
—Psalm 89:15

An Affirmation of Faith

In the name of Jesus I walk through life exalting Your Word.

Then he said: "The God of our fathers has chosen you to know his will and to see the Righteous One and to hear words from his mouth."
—*Acts 22:14*

For who has known the mind of the Lord that he may instruct him? But we have the mind of Christ.
—*1 Corinthians 2:16*

An Affirmation of Steadfastness

Lord, let me walk my life upon the foundation of Your Word.

A Woman's Prayer Journal

Have you ever wondered whether there is more spiritual life than you are currently experiencing? For most, the answer is usually, "Yes." It is perfectly fine and, I think, natural to expect something deeper, richer, and more profound from your spiritual life and a more complete experience of prayer is the key to realizing it. Use these pages to keep a journal about your new life of prayer. Write down whom or what you are praying for and use it as both a reminder and a way to stay on a prayerful track.

_____

_____

_____

_____

_____

_____

_____

_____

_____

_____

_____

_____

"Heaven is full of answers to prayer for which no one bothered to ask."

Rev. Billy Graham

_____

_____

_____

_____

_____

_____

_____

_____

_____

_____

_____

"Prayer requires more of the heart than of the tongue."

Adam Clarke

_____

_____

_____

_____

_____

_____

_____

_____

_____

_____

_____

_____

"We must move from asking God to take care of the things that are breaking our hearts, to praying about the things that are breaking His heart."

Margaret Gibb

"Prayer is exhaling the spirit of man and inhaling the spirit of God."

Edwin Keith

About the Author

John Bright-Fey teaches classes on prayer, contemplation, and leading a prayerful life. He is the author of several books in the Morning Cup and Whole Heart series. He lives in Birmingham, Alabama.

You may also enjoy these other devotionals in the Morning Cup series. Each one would be a welcomed and treasured gift for the special people in your life.

A Morning Cup of® Prayer for Teachers

ISBN-13: 978-1-57587-265-0
ISBN-10: 1-57587-265-X

A Morning Cup of® Prayer for Mothers

ISBN-13: 978-1-57587-264-3
ISBN-10: 1-57587-264-1

A Morning Cup of® Prayer for Friends

ISBN-13: 978-1-57587-263-6
ISBN-10: 1-57587-263-3

Prayer at a Glance

Prayer is talking with God

- Anytime
- Anywhere
- Under any circumstance
- About anything
- Authentically

 Step One: Set the stage with solitude, silence, and stillness.

 Step Two: Embrace a prayerful attitude.

 Step Three: Choose your method of prayer.

 Step Four: Talk with God.

 Step Five: Listen to God.

Tear this page out and post it in a handy spot for quick reference to help you make time to pray.